BOX OF CHOCOLATES

BOX OF CHOCOLATES

*Assorted Poems for
Assorted Times*

DONALD T. IANNONE

Wisdom Work Press

To every soul navigating the labyrinth of life's grand farce,
Where logic falters and reason dances askew—
This is for us, the brave wayfarers of the bizarre,
Grasping for meaning in the theater of the absurd.

ACKNOWLEDGMENTS

Poets, the alchemists of thought, wield their words to unravel our tight grip on the pedestrian. In a time gasping for breath under the weight of relentless absurdity, nonlinearity, and uncertainty, poetry emerges as the defibrillator for our numbed senses. It jolts us awake, challenging us to perceive and endure life's tumult with fresh, unclouded eyes. These literary mavericks serve as both the force that disrupts our slumber and the gentle guide leading us into the terra incognita of tomorrow. This anthology pays homage to the bards who dare to disrupt, to comfort, and to escort us across the threshold of the known, into the vast potential of 'what could be.' Among such visionary voices are the likes of Maya Angelou, with her incisive revelations of human nature; T.S. Eliot, who mapped the wastelands of modernity; Langston Hughes, who captured the vibrant thrum of cultural change; and Sylvia Plath, who dissected the psyche with surgical precision. Each, in their own unique cadence, shakes us, stirs us, and shepherds us into the unfolding enigma of the future.

WISDOM WORK PRESS

At Wisdom Work Press, we define wisdom as the conscious integration of knowledge, experience, reflective understanding, and a measured tolerance for life's uncertainties and its continuous changes. Personal wisdom is most important, which requires self-knowledge, discipline, and self-leadership. These qualities ensure that we walk the wisdom path through life. Our publications and services help others to discover and mount their wisdom paths in life. We are located in Chagrin Falls, Ohio. Website: https://wisdomworkpress.wordpress.com/

CONTENTS

In the face of an uncertain and broken world, poetry emerges as a transformative force, igniting the fires of compassion, truth, and empathy. In these desperate times, when extremism, hatred, prejudice, deceit, and selfishness seem to prevail, the world needs poetry more than ever. Amidst the chaos and confusion, poetry serves as a sanctuary for those seeking solace, inspiration, and a deeper understanding of the human experience. It weaves words into a tapestry of profound meaning, capturing the essence of our shared struggles and triumphs. Poetry gives a voice to the unheard, empowering the silenced and marginalized. Through its evocative verses, poetry transcends the limitations of language, touching the depths of our souls with its raw honesty. It offers comfort in times of despair, resilience in the face of adversity, and hope when all seems lost. In the embrace of poetry, individuals find the armor they need to navigate the treacherous terrain of our world, emerging stronger, wiser, and ready to face whatever challenges lie ahead.

The poems in this diverse collection serve as reminders to look beyond ourselves and our narrow perspectives, embracing the broader context of our existence. They remind us to see the world's beauty, laugh at its absurdities, and use our imaginations to envision a better world.

~Don Iannone

Box of Chocolates

life's a curious box of chocolates
(bittersweet, and nutty at the core)
in the wrappings of days, we find
assorted moments (fleeting, lingering)

we bite into mornings not knowing
(surprise! a hint of almond or apricot)
will today melt like caramel
or snap like dark chocolate's sharp retort?

nougat-thick are the evenings
filled with the chewy texture of thought
(what if, and maybe) swirling in coffee-dipped dreams
while the world spins in syrupy knots

and here we are, picking through
not by the guide (lost it, we did)
but by feel and by taste and by daring
(a gamble, a risk, a bet on living)

crunchy are these times, sprinkled with sea salt tears
(glisten, they do, on the wrapper of now)
but oh, how rich is the box of chocolates
with no two the same (uncertain and wild and wow)

for every bite, though unsure,
brings a flavor all its own
in this world of ours
(every taste, a poem)

Peeing in Cups

In a urologist's office, a sight so absurd,
A crowd of grown men, their bladders all stirred,
In the restroom they gathered, cups in their hand,
To pee for their doctors, in this puzzling land.

> With tiny plastic cups, they aimed to comply,
> In pursuit of their health, no need to be shy,
> Each man took his turn, with a humorous glance,
> Filling those cups, in a peculiar dance.

> The sound of their streams, like a symphony played,
> As they aimed for the target, their faces displayed,
> A mix of embarrassment, laughter, and grace,
> In this odd situation, they found their own space.

> The cups filled up quickly, in this comic routine,
> As the men peed for science, their faces turned green,
> But the urologist smiled, with a nod and a wink,
> For their dedication to health, he'd buy them a drink.

So in that small restroom, with cups all around,
A crowd of brave men, in this spectacle they found,
A humorous moment, in life's quirky parade,
Where dignity's price tag, in laughter, was paid.

Poetry as Armor in an Imperiled World

i carry your words
like a suit of armor,
a shield against the arrows
of a world in disarray.

letters dance upon my skin,
forming a tapestry of solace,
weaving threads of resilience
in the face of adversity.

in this fragmented existence,
where chaos reigns supreme,
i find refuge in the lines,
the pauses, the spaces between.

words become my sanctuary,
a fortress of ink and thought,
where i am safe from the storms
that threaten to consume.

with each verse,
i forge a path forward,
defying the odds,
defying the tempest's fury.

for poetry is my resolute armor,
my refuge, my steadfast guide,
as i navigate this tumultuous world
that seeks to break my stride.

so let the winds howl,
let the darkness descend,
i shall stand tall,
protected by the power of words.

The Poet's Sword

In the realm of steel and fire,
Where valor meets its burning pyre,
A poet wields a sacred blade,
A weapon forged, a verse conveyed.

With ink and quill, the poet's might,
Transcends the realm of mortal fight.
Each stroke, a thrust, a strike of words,
A symphony of battle chords.

This poet's sword, a cherished art,
A masterpiece, a work of heart.
Its hilt adorned with gems and gold,
A tale of legends yet untold.

With every line, the sword takes flight,
Unsheathed, it pierces through the night.
Its blade, a beacon in the haze,
A guide through darkness, vibrant blaze.

In times of turmoil and despair,
This poet's sword, a shield to bear.
It cuts through doubt, it vanquishes fear,
Its presence bold, its purpose clear.

For in the poet's hand it rests,
A symbol of strength, its blade blessed.
With every stroke, it carves a path,
A testament to the poet's wrath.

So raise your pens, ye poets bold,
Let your words be swords untold.
For in your verses, passions rise,
And in your lines, the spirit flies.

Embrace the power of the poet's sword,
With honor, courage, never bored.
For in its artistry, we find,
A world of beauty, unconfined.

Let the poet's sword forever reign,
A symbol of art's eternal domain.
In ink and steel, let us unite,
And wield our words with all our might.

Skin

Consider the skin,
that faithful sentinel,
a parchment of existence,
a canvas of life's artistry.

It is the first to greet the morning sun,
the last to bid the moon goodnight,
a silent witness to the world,
recording each touch, each caress,
each sting of winter's icy breath.

It is the boundary of our being,
the edge of our universe,
a map of our journey,
etched with lines of laughter and sorrow,
a testament to our resilience.

It is the keeper of our secrets,
the armor of our vulnerability,
a cloak of many colors,
woven with threads of identity,
a tapestry of our human story.

It is the language of our bodies,
the poetry of our existence,
a symphony of sensation,
playing the music of touch,
a dance of life on the stage of the world.

So let us honor our skin,
this extraordinary garment,
this living, breathing masterpiece,
for it is more than just a covering,
it is the essence of our humanity,
the signature of our soul.

Whispers of Forgotten Voices

In the hush of an ancient bookstore's chamber,
A dim light gently touched the aging wood,
Where rested a leather-bound journal, worn by time,
Its yellowed pages cradling dreams and musings.

A long-forgotten writer's essence dwelled within,
Their words, a timeless echo in the silent air,
As curious fingertips traced the fading ink,
A connection forged to thoughts; emotions bared.

Though the author's name had vanished in obscurity,
Their spirit lingered, an unbroken thread,
In the delicate dance of ink and paper's embrace,
A testament to words, in books unread.

This scene, a poignant reminder etched in time,
Of language's enduring power, its artful spell,
In the pages of a journal, a lasting rhyme,
Symbolic immortality, where stories dwell.

Surviving in the Post-Truth World

In the realm of post-truth and misinformation,
We find ourselves adrift on a turbulent sea,
Deceit's waves rise, falsehoods obscure the sun,
Facts, like elusive phantoms, fade from view.

This treacherous current, a serpent coiled,
Around the pillars of reason, constricts our grasp,
Threatening to engulf our collective thought,
As we navigate murky waters of manipulation.

The lighthouse of objective reality stands,
Obscured by the fog of deceit, doubt's embrace,
Sirens of disinformation sing beguiling songs,
In this distorted reflection of truth, we dwell.

We, the sailors of the digital age, must wield,
The compass of critical thought to chart,
A course toward distant shores of clarity,
Across this tempestuous sea of ambiguity.

Dysfunctional Families

In the heart of a dysfunctional family, roots run deep,
Entwined with threads of unresolved struggles, secrets buried,
The branches of generational strife, heavy with history,
Stretch across time, bearing the weight of ancient sorrows.

Communication, like a labyrinth, twists and turns,
Misunderstandings woven into the very fabric of existence,
Conflict, a constant companion in this fractured world,
Where wounds fester, and healing is a distant dream.

The impact reverberates through lives, a haunting echo,
Leaving scars etched deep, like tattoos of pain,
Emotional legacies, like heirlooms passed down,
Shaping minds, molding hearts, defining destinies.

Yet, within the chaos, resilience may arise,
A spark of hope, a longing for transformation,
Like a fragile shoot breaking through hardened soil,
Reaching for the warmth of a distant sun.

Narrative Journeys

In the vast expanse of our existential lives,
We confront the profound, elusive question of meaning,
Wandering through a boundless desert of existence,
Seeking purpose amidst shifting sands and endless horizons.

Within us, an innate yearning stirs,
A deep desire to grasp our place in the cosmic scheme,
To unravel the enigma of our fleeting existence,
To plumb the depths of our existence's essence.

Some venture into the labyrinth of philosophy,
Delving into the intricacies of thought and wisdom's realm,
While others find solace in the sanctuary of faith,
Seeking meaning in the whispers of the spiritual.

In the tapestry of life, connections are woven,
Moments of love and human touch, threads of significance,
And in the face of life's inscrutable mysteries,
We are entrusted with crafting our own narratives and meanings.

Amelia Island Ballet

As the sun dips low on the horizon's edge,
Gilding the sands of Amelia Island with its radiance,
The waves, relentless, rhythmic, arrive.
Each swell, a breath drawn deep from the sea's vast soul,
Gathering momentum, gathering power,
Unfurls gracefully, a white lace from an ancient azure tapestry.

Thunderous applause, they crash upon the shore,
A timeless dance between land and sea,
And in their retreat, they offer treasures—
A gleaming, jeweled trove, whispered secrets from the deep.

This, the eternal ballet of Amelia,
Where ocean's poetry meets earth's embrace,
Every wave, a verse, in nature's grand narrative.

Lightning Strike

Deep within the forest's sacred sanctuary,
Beneath the towering canopy of ancient sentinels,
Celestial fury, like a sudden revelation, descends.
A brilliant sear, a sun-like blaze,
Lightning strikes, fierce and untamed,
Choosing its arboreal vessel with divine precision.

    A jagged vein, a celestial sword,
    Cleaves the heavens, sundering earth and sky,
    A thunderous clap, an echo through the woods,
    Shaking the very roots of ancient wisdom.

The oak, once unwavering, now bears the scars,
Its gnarled limbs smoldering, its trunk charred,
A testament to nature's capricious dance.
Yet, even in its fiery destruction, an eerie beauty remains.

    An intricate fractal etched by lightning's hand,
    A tapestry of tendrils and veins,
    A sacred dialogue between sky and earth,
    In the heart of the forest's enduring mystery.

Stories that Books Tell

In twilight's hushed embrace,
The book begins its tale,
Pages unfurl like a maestro's hand,
Guiding a silent symphony.

From the parchment, words ascend,
Dancing secrets, whispers sent,
Around the edges of the mind,
Heartstrings pulled in gentle kind.

These are not mere tales retold,
But dreams in vivid emotion molded,
Carrying one to unknown spaces,
Beyond the bounds of familiar places.

Chapters move in graceful flow,
While paragraphs their stories show,
Sentences weave a tapestry bright,
Stories of wonder, taking flight.

In this moment, brief and still,
The book lives, feels, and will,
Share with us, in every detail,
The heartbeats of its timeless tale.

Pileated Woodpecker

Amidst the silent whisper of woods,
The pileated woodpecker's drumming echoed,
Piercing the hush with rhythmic intent.
Its crimson crest, a vivid flame,
Bobbed fervently on decayed canvas.

Each strike,
A shower of bark and fragments,
Revealing skeletal remains of ancient timber.

Monochromatic plumage,
Black and white against mossy greens,
A stark artist amidst nature's hues.

Sunlight filters, dappled shadows play,
In tandem with fervent pecks,
A tableau of life and decay
In the forest's embrace.

Lone Dandelion

In a verdant meadow expanse,
A lone dandelion stands,
Trading golden crown
For a halo of fragile wisps.

Sun's affection now distant,
Yet in its fragile state,
An ethereal beauty emerges,
An elder amidst fleeting youth.

Holding a thousand dreams,
Awaiting the gust's embrace,
Whispered tales ready to be shared,
With an ever-changing world.

Silent beacon it remains,
Testament to resilience and phases,
Embracing life's ebb and flow,
In the dance of time and change.

Delicate Dance

In a corner softly illuminated,
The weight of yesteryears presses.
An old man, hands trembling,
Carrying the topography of decades,
Holds a fading quill.

The inkwell, as profound
As memories entombed,
Yet each touch to parchment falters,
Betraying the battles within.

Words, once rivers, now
Stagnate — dammed by time's relentless sands.
Eyes clouded, but with sparks of resolve,
They search,
Delve into mind's caverns
For the perfect sentiment's echo.

Stuttering starts, lines retraced,
Each pause heavy
With a life's symphony of emotions.
He is reminded,
Of the delicate dance between
Beauty's poignancy and creation's pain.

Chagrin Falls

In the fold of Ohio's green embrace,
Chagrin Falls —
A dream caught in the gossamer of time.
Waterfall's grace,
Deceptive in its power,
Whispers tales of pioneers, of ancient mills,
Setting the town's pulse.

Cobblestone veins,
Lined with memory's boutiques, cafes with stories,
Hum with life's subtle breath.
Each stone cradling footprints,
Echoing laughter, secrets unveiled.

Nostalgia clings to the village air,
Wooden beams, brick facades
Soaked in moments now shadows.
Walking here is a journey
Through history's tactile pages,
Fragrant with blossoms,
Tinged with distant bells.

Chagrin Falls,
A convergence of past and present,
Invites hearts to its canvas,
Where epochs waltz
In an unending embrace.

Martins Ferry

Martins Ferry,
Cradled by the winding Ohio River,
Unfolds as a luminous tapestry
Of epochs past,
And the fragile flicker of dreams yet to be told.

Its streets, echoing
The metallic chorus of yesteryears,
The steel mills, the coal mines,
Are now flanked by brick guardians.
Their faces, maps of time,
Bear the chronicles of both sweat and spirit.

Each corner holds a tale:
Ancient lampposts with their pools of golden memory,
Gardens, which against all odds,
Bloom between stone and shadow.

The river, that glassy scribe,
Reflects the ever-changing ballet above,
Clouds drifting,
Azure stretching,
Whispering the town's secrets,
Its fervent wishes.

And within these boundaries,
A kinship pulses.
In the tender greetings exchanged at dawn,
The wisdom traded under a canopy of stars,
The laughter, free and uninhibited,
Bouncing off walls that have seen generations.

Martins Ferry,
More than mere coordinates on a map,
Is a living narrative,
A dance between its storied past
And the promise of many tomorrows.

Sedona

Sedona,
Red rocks ascend,
Sky stretches, vast.

Whispers linger,
Sun graces peaks,
Shadows dance.

Amidst juniper,
Desert's touch,
Land sings.

Vortices spin,
Seekers drawn,
Sacred ground.

Where earth meets divine,
Nature, spirit,
Magic surrounds.

Mississippi River

Mississippi River,
Majestic serpentine ribbon,
Carving through America's lush tapestry.

Age-old murmurs,
Beneath the shadows of towering cottonwoods,
Under the ballet of kaleidoscopic skies.

Each undulating ripple,
A vivid narrative,
Moments held in shimmering touch.

Flowing, ever meandering,
A timeless testament,
Its waters a rich chronicle.

Bridging amber North to emerald South,
Mingling tales of golden past and iridescent present,
A pulsating lifeline, a watchful guardian,
In its ceaseless, unyielding vigil.

Florida Keys

Florida Keys,
Cascade of jade and coral,
Laid beneath the cerulean gaze
Of a sea kissed by tangerine rays.

Dancing,
An ageless rhythm of tides,
Where molten sun blankets opalescent depths,
Ebony palm shadows intersect with turquoise ebbs.

Isles unfold,
From Key West's bustling fervor and fiery retreats,
To Big Pine's tranquil lavender embrace.
Murmured tales emerge,
Of pirates draped in crimson,
Poets with cerulean gaze,
Emerald-lit midnight dances.

On this edge,
Where amber horizon meets indigo dreams,
Silver-winged seabirds rise,
Carrying whispers of sapphire twilights
And the promise of amethyst mornings.

Lessons from a Mirror

In the bedroom's dim light,
She stood,
Eyes fixed on the mirror.
The glass told truths,
Revealed lines and creases,
Marks of years, of life.

Her fingers touched memories,
Youth, vigor,
Days long gone.
But her eyes held strength,
Seeing every scar, every wrinkle,
Understanding the tales they told.

There,
She recognized her journey,
Mapped on skin,
Silent,
Resilient,
Enduring.

Losing a Best Friend

In the waning light,
A girl stands removed, observing.
A man, with deliberate tenderness,
Touches the weary form of his dog, his best friend.

The world narrows to this moment,
Hands full of memories,
Tracing lifelines of an aging companion.
The weight of fleeting time palpable.

She feels, from a distance,
The pull of an ending,
The quiet grief of love's ebb,
Two souls, bound in silent understanding.

Memories in the Embers

In the wide stretch of country,
A house's remains, charred and alone,
Stand against golden wheat fields,
Its beams, blackened and frail,
Reaching for the blue sky.

The ground holds the scent
Of fire and old memories,
Yet, nearby, wildflowers brave the ash,
Blooming in defiant color.

The meadow's wind carries whispers,
Stories of a warmth once there,
Of laughter, now stilled,
Echoes fading in the vast, open land.

The Calf and the Butterfly

In the midst of barnyard hum,
A Holstein calf rests,
Black and white against green pasture,
Eyes fixed on a yellow-tailed butterfly.

The butterfly, light and fleeting,
Finds warmth on the calf's muzzle,
And sometimes, a gentle perch
Against those large, curious eyes.

Afternoons stretch long,
With the calf's breath lifting the butterfly,
And the butterfly, in return,
Dancing a silent waltz of gratitude.

Two worlds meet,
Ephemeral touches enduring,
In the quiet dance
Of the unexpected.

Chicago: Crucible of Toil and Grace

Chicago, in days of yore, a city of towering dreams,
Where steel and stone painted the sky's canvas,
Cobblestone streets, the vivacious clatter of streetcars' schemes,
Resounded with immigrant voices, a kaleidoscope of you and I.

Speakeasies hummed with jazz's sultry, smoky refrain,
In the hues of saxophones and trumpets' golden light,
The stockyards' clatter, a beastly, thunderous mane,
Amidst the factories' relentless fire, a symphony in the night.

The Chicago River, a serpentine ribbon, a silver vein,
Wove through the heart, reflecting dreams in shimmering gleam,
In this city of sweat, of hope that would sustain,
In the land of the brave and the audacious dream.

Chicago, forged in a crucible of toil and grace,
A city where progress and passion fused, a vibrant embrace,
A testament to the human spirit's colorful chase,
In your arms, old Chicago, we find our place.

New Roof

Beneath the late October sky,
Warm hues of autumn softly kiss,
An army of Guatemalan workers,
Their mission clear, their movements precise.

    In denim and sun-bleached shirts,
    They march, a seasoned battalion,
    Pounding hammers, riveting drills,
    Their symphony of labor echoing.

Tools clash and meld with the scent,
Of fresh-cut timber, earthy and robust,
Each tile, a careful stroke on canvas,
A masterpiece of resilience and craft.

    Amidst laughter and shared camaraderie,
    Their Spanish volleys harmonize,
    The roof transforms, a quiet testament,
    To their skill and unwavering dedication,
    Under the ever-shifting Northeast Ohio sky.

A Late October Feast

Picture a dinner, a feast for the senses,
With a tender pork loin, seasoned, succulent,
Stuffed with herbs and cheese, flavors emerge,
Each bite, a culinary voyage, an enticing surge.

Sweet potatoes, roasted, their skins crisp,
Topped with bacon, cheese, sour cream's bliss,
Soft, caramelized interiors, a delightful twist,
A medley of textures, flavors persist.

Grilled asparagus, a touch of the grill's kiss,
Drizzled with olive oil, a verdant bliss,
Fresh-baked rolls, warm, inviting to savor,
Butter's embrace, a comforting flavor.

A wine, thoughtfully paired, enhances the scene,
Notes and aromas, a gastronomic dream,
This dinner, a symphony, a culinary delight,
An exquisite banquet, a memorable night.

The Fat Man and His Elephant

In the heart of the bustling circus tent,
A lone spotlight bathes the scene in its soft light,
A rotund man, adorned in lively attire,
Perches atop a majestic elephant.

His generous form is a tapestry of colors,
A costume that sparkles and shimmers,
On the back of the regal pachyderm,
He sits like a king on his throne.

The elephant, a creature of wisdom and grace,
Bears the weight of the man with ease,
Moving with deliberate and elegant strides,
Creating a harmonious spectacle beneath the big top.

The audience watches in wonder and amazement,
As this unlikely pair takes center stage,
The plump man and the colossal beast,
Unite to embody the magic of the circus.

The Unexpected at Yankee Stadium

At Yankee Stadium, so vast and grand,
A hot air balloon, off-course, did land,
Its colors vibrant, like a comet it appeared,
Disrupting the game, as the crowd all peered.

Mickey Mantle, a legend, poised just right,
Swung his bat with all his might,
Cheers from the stands, electric and loud,
As the baseball soared into the cloud.

But fate had a twist, a surprise in store,
The balloon crashed down with a mighty roar,
The baseball collided, a spectacle to be,
As destiny and chance converged, you see.

In the annals of Yankee lore, this tale's been spun,
A collision of worlds beneath the summer sun,
Where rhyme and reason, chance and fate,
Created a moment none could anticipate.

A Second Take on Christ's Second Coming

In the wake of Christ's Second Coming, a spectacle unfurled,
A cosmic transformation, a dance of a cosmic world,
The world bathed in the brilliance of His divine light,
A profound shift, both day and night.

Sinners, once ensnared in the chains of their dark past,
Now drawn, like moths to a celestial fire, at last,
Towards the Holy Gate, an ethereal, beckoning guide,
Their hearts and souls reborn on this sacred ride.

The weight of their transgressions, like shadows, fade away,
As each step towards salvation's path they sway,
A metamorphosis profound, of guilt's release,
They walk the radiant path to eternal peace.

Forgiveness, like a healing balm, soothes their souls,
Divine love's embrace, their once-tattered hearts console,
In this cosmic moment, redemption takes the stage,
As sinners find themselves embraced by Heaven's sage.

The Holy Gate, a portal to a world unknown,
Where grace and mercy in boundless rivers have flown,
An awakening, a transformation, a sacred decree,
As sinners become part of Heaven's grand tapestry.

In this story of the Second Coming's cosmic design,
The sinful and redeemed unite, a union so divine,
Their journey of redemption, an odyssey of grace,
As they enter the realm of eternity's warm embrace.

The Hippie's Wild Rhino Ride through Chagrin Falls

In Chagrin Falls, where quiet streets wind,
A tale unfolds, both quirky and kind,
In a town so creative, historic, and refined,
Where affluence and charm beautifully bind.

Amidst the hush of the tranquil lanes,
An old hippie embarked on his unique domains,
With a beard so long, like wisps of cloud,
He rode a blue rhino, odd but proud.

Almost naked, just a tie-dyed wrap,
Through the town's historic heart, he'd adapt,
Down quaint streets with creative flair,
In a place where history lingered in the air.

The rhino, a legend, both strange and profound,
Moved gracefully through this affluent town,
As people gathered in awe, their laughter set free,
In a place that treasures eccentricity so happily.

Flocks of people watched on, spellbound and keen,
Taking it as a sign, an unusual scene,
That Hell, most surely, was freezing over with Mitchell's ice cream,
In this town, where life's mysteries they'd dream.

In Chagrin Falls, where past and present unite,
The old hippie's journey, a whimsical sight,
In this quiet, creative, historic domain,
He reminded us to question and not just restrain.

Louie Armstrong and His Polka-Dot Giraffe

In the heart of Chicago, one sunny day,
Louie Armstrong came out to play,
With his trumpet in hand, and a gleam in his eye,
He mounted his giraffe, polka-dotted and spry.

With a toot and a holler, they started to roll,
Down the bustling streets, a sight to behold,
The giraffe's spots danced in a whimsical way,
As Louie's horn serenaded the city with a jazzy display.

People looked up, their jaws to the floor,
As Louie played tunes they'd never heard before,
The giraffe pranced and twirled with a joyful demeanor,
In this musical escapade, they were the city's main arena.

They paraded through parks, and by the lakeside,
With Louie's horn, there was no place to hide,
The city echoed with laughter and cheer,
As Louie and his giraffe brought smiles near and clear.

Through skyscrapers and alleys, they made their grand tour,
A jazz-infused spectacle, of that, you can be sure,
In the heart of Chicago, that vibrant town,
Louie Armstrong's polka-dot giraffe wore a jazzy crown.

Jackal and Pride

In a land of laughter and peculiar delight,
Lived Dr. Sylvester Jackal, an odd but brilliant sight,
With a lab coat askew and goggles on his head,
He concocted strange potions in his laboratory shed.

By his side was Remus Pride, his trusty comrade true,
A mischievous grin, always ready with a clue,
With a twinkle in his eye and a chuckle in his throat,
They embarked on adventures, with stories to promote.

Dr. Jackal's inventions, a cacophony of quirk,
From a self-peeling banana to a motorized fork,
They left people puzzled, amazed, and amused,
In the realm of oddity, they truly excelled and enthused.

One day they built a rocket, quite a sight to behold,
But it only flew backward, or so I've been told,
They laughed it off heartily, as they often would do,
For in their world of whimsy, every mishap was true.

From bubblegum bridges to jellybean cars,
Their escapades took them to the moon and to Mars,
With Remus by his side, and laughter as their guide,
Dr. Jackal and his sidekick, forever side by side.

So here's to the duo, with humor as their pride,
In a world of jest and laughter, they'd forever reside,
Dr. Jackal and Remus, a pair like no other,
Their comical tales, a bond we'll always smother.

A Ball for Left-Footed Debutantes

In the realm of the absurd, where chaos takes the lead,
Debutantes with two left feet gather for a peculiar need,
A ball for the awkward, a dance for those askew,
Their hearts belong to bowling, and poison ivy they grew.

Gloved hands clutching ball and pins, shuffling through the night,
Twisting, turning, twirling wrong, with all their left-foot might,
Gowns of lace and satin, embellished, but in vain,
For elegance escapes their grasp, like drops of summer rain.

In their English gardens, where blooms should softly sway,
They nurture poison ivy, in a most peculiar way,
Their love for the sinister, the awkward, and the strange,
Defines this curious debutante ball's deranged range.

They waltz amidst the bowling lanes, where pins become their foes,
As laughter echoes loudly, their toes collide in rows,
With graceless spins and clumsy grace, they find a quirky blend,
In a world where oddity and charm, with missteps, freely blend.

So raise a glass to debutantes, the ones who boldly dare,
To dance their dance with two left feet, in gowns beyond compare,
For in their love for bowling and ivy's creeping green,
They weave a tapestry of whimsy, a sight to be seen.

Bewitched Old Women
with Cheshire Smiles

Where whimsy and wonder unite,
Lived old women with Cheshire smiles, a bewitching sight,
Their ample bosoms, like mountains they'd rise,
To tempt young men, with curious eyes.

With grace they'd saunter, in gardens they'd roam,
Their bosoms their treasure, their secrets their own,
But young men, oh so curious and sly,
Would sneak peeks, with a twinkle in eye.

With a wink and a grin, they'd ponder and think,
"We'll teach them a lesson, both cunning and pink,
In realms of enchantment, their stories unfold,
In worlds where whimsy and secrets are gold."

So, curses they'd cast, like spells from a dream,
Sending young men into realms that made them scream,
Through rhubarb jungles and dandelion seas,
In a world filled with wonders and endless tease.

In this whimsical realm, where tales take flight,
These old women with Cheshire smiles, a mesmerizing sight,
They'd paint their own stories, both wily and keen,
In a land where curiosity reigns, evergreen.

Yoga in the Petunias and Peonies

In petunias and peonies, a sight so surreal,
Yoga enthusiasts, on nature's tranquil wheel,
They twisted and stretched in this floral domain,
In a pose-filled pursuit of serenity's gain.
Downward dog amidst daisies, a warrior with the rose,
In the garden of namaste, their passion freely flows,
The sun salutation met the morning glories high,
As they breathed in the fragrance 'neath the cerulean sky.
Lotus blooms became their peaceful retreat,
While the hummingbirds whispered, "Isn't this sweet?"
Warblers, their gurus, in the treetops so tall,
Guided them in poses, from tree to waterfall.
With butterflies as partners in their graceful ballet,
They danced 'mongst the dahlias, in the soft light of day,
And as twilight descended, in the garden they'd rest,
In a savasana slumber, 'midst blossoms so blessed.
So in petunias and peonies, they'd stretch and they'd sigh,
With laughter and balance, reaching for the sky,
In this whimsical yoga, in the heart of their bloom,
They found peace 'mongst the petals, in nature's grand room.

Selected Haiku Poems

Selected Haikus

Sacred cows beware,
Irreverence fills the air,
Laughter beyond care.

Traffic jam ahead,
Bananas in my backpack,
Life's odd twists, misled.

Big butts in motion,
Shaking with sheer devotion,
Booty's wild ocean.

Man's big red nose glows,
Laughter follows where he goes,
Clowning, he bestows.

Crooked Zen master,
Teaching life's bends and fractures,
Wisdom's strange master.

Jamaican sausage,
Spicier than a fire-breathing llama,
Flavor explosion!

Tibetan Monks at Madison Square Garden

Three monks from Tibet, robes a vivid hue,
Found themselves lost in a boisterous zoo,
At Madison Square Garden, they wandered astray,
Amidst the boxing fervor, they decided to stay.

Their saffron robes fluttered, as they looked around,
In a sea of excitement, where punches resound,
With puzzled expressions, they sought to divine,
The purpose of pugilists in a squared line.

They marveled at fighters, with gloves in a fuss,
Unleashing their punches, creating a fuss,
In this world of fisticuffs, fierce and so wild,
The monks found enlightenment, amidst punches piled.

With humor in hearts, they cheered and they jeered,
At the boxing spectacle, their voices revered,
In iambic tetrameter, their laughter did bloom,
Three Tibetan monks in Madison's grand room.

The Devil Made Me Do It

The Devil made me do it, I swear it's true,
He whispered temptations, what could I do?
He offered me cookies, both warm and sweet,
And said, "Just one won't hurt, it's a tiny treat."

He danced in my dreams, with a mischievous grin,
Said, "Skip that workout, let laziness win."
He tempted me with Netflix, one more episode,
And promised tomorrow, I'd hit the road.

The Devil made me do it, he led me astray,
Said, "Skip the salad, have dessert today."
He urged me to procrastinate, just a bit longer,
And before I knew it, my to-do list grew stronger.

But as I gave in to his cunning persuasion,
I couldn't help but find some consolation,
For in life's mischief and moments askew,
I discovered laughter, and a chuckle or two.

So, blame it on the Devil, that sly, wicked sprite,
For leading us astray, both day and night,
In his temptations and tricks, we sometimes find,
A humorous twist to life's daily grind.

Red and Gray Barn in Autumn

Hallowed
Standing all alone,
Lonely, worn dirt road,
Autumn's almost barren face.

Faded red and gray,
Empty now, longing for love,
Weathered wood, a rich history told,
Mature grace in its simplicity.

Dried grassy fields about,
Frozen in time,
Harvest past, soon winter.

Lingering gray-white fog,
Gathered forebodingness,
In this moment, time stands still.

The Paradox of a Pair of Ducks

Paradox, a waltzing enigma,
Twirls with a pair of ducks,
In a dance of contradictions,
Where meaning and absurdity intermingle.

Their steps, a tango of paradox,
Graceful yet disorienting,
A juxtaposition of logic and whimsy,
A riddle that defies comprehension.

Paradox leads, with a mischievous grin,
As the ducks follow, quacking in rhythm,
Their feathers a riot of contrasting hues,
Reflecting the paradoxical nature of existence.

In this dance, opposites converge,
Harmony and chaos, order and disorder,
A swirling vortex of contradictions,
Where certainty and uncertainty collide.

Oh, Ezra Pound, master of the enigmatic,
Would revel in this dance of paradox,
Finding beauty in the inexplicable,
And meaning in the dance of the ducks.

For in the paradoxical embrace,
We glimpse the complexity of life,
And find solace in the mystery,
As the ducks and paradox continue to dance.

The Pencil

a pencil, slender and sleek,
whispers secrets on the page,
its graphite tip, a dancer's toe,
tracing lines of thought, unencumbered.

it dances across the paper's stage,
twirling and swirling in graceful arcs,
a silent symphony of words and shapes,
unfolding the mysteries of the mind.

its lead, a conductor's baton,
conducting the orchestra of ideas,
scribbling melodies of inspiration,
in the language of graphite and wood.

oh, pencil, humble and unassuming,
you hold the power to create,
to give life to thoughts and dreams,
with each stroke, a world takes shape.

so let us cherish this simple tool,
this wand of possibility and expression,
for in its simplicity, it holds the key,
to unlock the wonders of imagination.

The Stockyard

In the heart of the city, the stockyard beats,
A pulsing rhythm of hooves and bleats.
Iron and steel, flesh and bone,
A symphony of life in monotone.

Cattle shuffle in endless lines,
Marked by numbers, devoid of signs.
Their eyes hold stories, tales untold,
In the stockyard's grip, a sight to behold.

The air is thick with dust and grime,
A testament to the march of time.
The sun sets low, casting long shadows,
Over the stockyard, where the cold wind blows.

Yet, in this place of iron and steel,
A certain truth begins to reveal.
Life and death, in a dance entwined,
In the stockyard's heart, a tale defined.

So let us not forget this place,
Where life unfolds at a steady pace.
For in its rhythm, raw and real,
The stockyard's heart, continues to feel.

Lone Sparrow

On a bare branch in winter,
a sparrow alights,
a small heart beating against the cold.

Oh, what a miracle to behold,
this tiny life in a world so vast,
a testament to the enduring song of survival.

She fluffs her feathers against the chill,
a soft armor against the winter's bite,
her song a spark in the silence,
a flame in the heart of the frost.

She does not ask for much,
just a perch to rest,
a seed to eat,
a moment of warmth in the sun.

And in her simplicity,
she teaches us,
that life is not about the grandeur,
but the quiet moments of being.

So let us learn from the sparrow,
humble poet of the winter branch,
for in her song, we find our own,
a melody of resilience, of hope, life.

Cancer

Consider cancer,
that unwelcome guest,
a shadow that creeps in uninvited,
a thief in the quiet of the night.

It is a cruel artist,
sketching its dark designs,
a silent scribe writing its story,
in the sacred text of our cells.

It is a relentless traveler,
journeying through the pathways of the body,
a nomad with no destination,
a wanderer with no home.

It is a paradox,
born of our own flesh and blood,
a traitor cloaked in familiarity,
a stranger wearing our own face.

Yet, in its presence, we find our strength,
a resilience we never knew we had,
a courage that rises like the dawn,
a light that refuses to be extinguished.

We become warriors, fighters, survivors,
our bodies the battlefield,
our spirit the weapon,
our hope the victory flag.

So let us honor those who battle,
who stand in the face of the storm,
for in their fight, we see our own,
a testament to the indomitable spirit of life.

Cancer may be a part of our story,
but it does not define us,
for we are more than our illness,
we are the poets of our own existence.

Lonely Pterodactyl

Consider the pterodactyl,
a lonely silhouette against the twilight sky,
a relic of a time long past,
a ghost in the grand theater of evolution.

He soars above the ancient earth,
his wings, vast canvases of leathery skin,
stretching out like the pages of a prehistoric tome,
each beat a verse in the epic of existence.

His cry echoes through the canyons,
a mournful aria in the symphony of survival,
a testament to his solitude,
a melody that dances with the wind.

He is a solitary sentinel,
a guardian of the primeval world,
his keen eyes scanning the landscape,
a silent observer of life's grand spectacle.

His world is one of towering ferns and colossal beasts,
a realm where giants roam and volcanoes roar,
a testament to nature's untamed power,
a canvas painted with the brush of time.

Yet, in his solitude, there is a certain grace,
a dignity that comes from enduring,
from soaring above the world, alone,
a testament to the resilience of life.

So let us honor the pterodactyl,
this lonely voyager of the ancient skies,
for in his story, we see our own,
a tale of survival, of endurance, of the will to fly.

Unfolding of a New Idea

a new idea
forms
in the quiet corners
of my mind
it whispers
softly
like a breeze
through an open window
it dances
with the shadows
of my thoughts
twisting and turning
in a delicate ballet
of possibility
the words
they come
in fragments
like scattered puzzle pieces
waiting to be assembled
into a coherent whole
the cadence
is a symphony
of irregular beats
a rhythm
that defies convention

and embraces the unexpected
the imagery
it blooms
like wildflowers
in a field
vibrant and untamed
painting pictures
with vivid strokes
the new idea
it takes shape
slowly
like a sunrise
unfolding
its colors
brightening the horizon
and as it grows
it fills me
with a sense
of wonder
of excitement
of endless potential
for in the sound and feel
of this new idea forming
I am reminded
of the beauty
of creation
and the power
of imagination.

A River Birch's
Outstretched Arms

In the heart of winter's grasp,
A solitary river birch stands guardian,
Its slender boughs, etched against the muted sky,
Dance a fragile ballet with the biting breeze.

Each branch, armored in a coat of ice and snow,
Clatters, not in defeat, but in whispered resistance,
Telling tales of seasons past and present,
Echoing the resilience of nature's timeless persistence.

The cold wind weaves through each twig and limb,
A spectral hand caressing the frozen silhouette,
As the birch quivers, each movement a testament,
To life's enduring spirit amidst winter's quiet threat.

Silvery bark peels in paper-thin layers,
Exposing the rawness beneath, tender and stark,
Yet, the birch stands, amidst snowflakes and frost,
A beacon of hope in the cold, desolate dark.

In this dance of shadows and winter's caress,
The clattering branches of the river birch sing,
A song of strength, of cycles, of life's fragile pace,
A reminder that even in stillness, there's an underlying spring.

A Streetcar from Long Ago

A steel behemoth in the city's flow,
Monstrous, yet graceful in its ponderous gait,
Through urban veins, it lumbers, firm and slow.

Its wheels, like ancient millstones, grind the track,
A rhythm in discord with city's haste,
In measured strides, it weaves through traffic's wrack.

The hum of cables sings an electric tune,
A tethered spiderweb above the fray,
Connecting nodes in this concrete cocoon.

Each window frames a world of transient lives,
Brief vignettes caught in moments as they pass,
In hidden dramas, subtle truth derives.

The streetcar's heart, a mechanical percussion,
A metronome of gears and pistons' might,
Yet within, passengers pulse in quiet discussion.

Beside, a beggar, with a cardboard plea,
A silent witness to the rolling scene,
His presence unnoticed, lost in reverie.

As twilight dims the city's ceaseless motion,
The streetcar carries stories, rich and stark,
A silent witness to this urban ocean.

In this symphony of steel, a paradox,
Precision in its chaos, wit in strife,
The streetcar plies its trade, unwavering, rocks.
A muted ballet on the asphalt stage,
In quiet grace, it carries lives unknown,
Through city streets, it writes its wordless page.

Pretty Boy

In the quiet corners of her room, she sits,
The grandmother, her hair a silver mist,
While time meanders, lost in memory's maze,
In her world, where shadows softly graze.

Beside her, perched upon a wooden rail,
A blue parakeet, his name is Pretty Boy,
With feathers bright, a sentinel so frail,
He watches, hints at life's elusive ploy.

With eyes that gleam like sapphires in the sun,
He fixes on her, knowing what must be done.
Precision in his movements, quick and spry,
He's her companion, whispering replies.

"Dear Pretty Boy," she murmurs with a sigh,
He tilts his head, a knowing in his eye,
He prompts her gently, with a tender cue,
"Morning awaits, the day's tasks to pursue."

He chirps and flutters, full of lively grace,
To guide her steps through each familiar space,
In his blue plumage, wisdom seems to hide,
A tiny oracle, perched by her side.

He calls her to the garden, bathed in light,
Where blossoms bloom, a vibrant, fragrant sight,
He nods towards the chores that must be done,
Reminding her, the day has just begun.

With each chirrup and flutter of his wings,
He stirs her soul, and to her heart, he clings,
He's more than just a parakeet, you see,
He's a messenger of her reality.

As evening falls, and shadows softly creep,
The grandmother, her eyes begin to weep,
Pretty Boy perches still, a steadfast friend,
In silence, they wait, until the day's end.

In this quiet dance, a delicate display,
Precision, wit, and wisdom's gentle sway,
A blue parakeet, with feathers bright and coy,
Whispers to the grandmother, her Pretty Boy.

Feeding a Stray Dog

In the stillness, on the weathered porch,
A stray dog, black and white, its eyes convey,
Approaches the elderly grandmother's chair,
With a heart heavy from life's weight.

He comes each day, a quiet companion,
To share a meal, a daily ritual,
An act of kindness, a soothing habit,
In life's relentless pace, a fleeting interlude.

His fur is coarse, his steps uncertain,
Yet he returns, gratitude evident,
Eyes telling stories of struggles endured,
A heart familiar with hunger and hardship.

No words pass between them in their routine,
Understanding flows without need for speech,
A bond unspoken but profoundly felt,
A connection transcending the passage of years.

He nuzzles her hand, a gentle gesture,
Expressing thanks for her unwavering care,
For the nourishment that eases his hunger,
In the fading light of her presence.

In their quiet moments, solace prevails,
An elderly grandmother, a stray companion,
Silent exchange of love, profound and unwavering,
Age and frailty dissolve in their connection.

Tanka and Haiku

Tanka
Knife carves wood with grace,
A boy whittling in the sun,
Crafting art from grain,
In his hands, stories take shape,
Wood whispers secrets, love flows.

Tanka
Winter moon so bright,
Casting silver on the snow,
Frozen world aglow,
In your tranquil, icy light,
Night's magic unfolds its show.

Tanka
Butterfly's breath,
Whispers on petals' grace,
Delicate threads,
Sustain beauty's fleeting flight,
Invisible, light as air.

Tanka
Butterfly's breath,
Whispers on petals' grace,
Delicate threads,

Sustain beauty's fleeting flight,
Invisible, light as air.

Haiku
Monk's laughter rings clear,
A serenely joyful sound,
Peace found in each note.

Haiku
Inhale, life begins,
Exhale, a world unfolds wide,
Breath, our constant guide.

Haiku
Dragonfly at rest,
On lily's leaf, serene perch,
Beauty in stillness.

Haiku
Hushed, deep,
Tranquil cloak,
Peace.

When a Clock's Hands
Move Backwards

In the realm of ticking time,
A clock, enchanted, takes its climb,
But not in the usual way we know,
For this clock moves backward, a mystical show.

Its hands reverse, with a gentle grace,
Turning back the years, erasing space,
And as it spins, a portal appears,
Inviting me to confront my deepest fears.

I step through the threshold, into the past,
A journey through time, memories amassed,
Each tick and tock, a whisper of yore,
Unveiling the lives I've lived before.

I wander through landscapes, foreign and strange,
Witnessing echoes of my soul's exchange,
In ancient realms, I was a warrior bold,
Fighting battles, stories yet untold.

In Renaissance hues, I was an artist's muse,
Inspiring masterpieces, love's sweet fuse,
And in the roaring twenties, I danced with glee,
A flapper, embracing life's jubilee.

Through the ages, I've worn many faces,
A seeker of truth in diverse places,
A healer, a teacher, a lover, a friend,
Each life a chapter, a tale to transcend.

As the clock winds back, I see the threads,
Connecting the lives, the paths I've tread,
Lessons learned, wisdom gained anew,
In each existence, a chance to renew.

But as the clock nears its final chime,
I realize the truth, transcending time,
That all these lives, though separate and vast,
Are but fragments of a soul that forever lasts.

For in this journey through my past,
I find the essence that will forever last,
A tapestry woven with love and strife,
A reminder of the eternal dance of life.

And as the clock returns to its steady beat,
I step back into the present, feeling complete,
For I carry within me the echoes of old,
A tapestry of lives, a story yet untold.

Ideation

ideas take off like rocket ships
into the boundless sky
with fiery tails and eager tips
they boldly aim so high

no rules or norms can hold them back
as they soar through the ether's track
defying gravity's earthly grip
ideas take off like rocket ships

      they start as sparks within the mind
      then gather fuel from dreams
      with inspiration intertwined
      they burst forth in great streams

      exploding into the unknown
      where endless possibilities are shown
      breaking free from earthly quips
      ideas take off like rocket ships

they pierce the heavens, reach the stars
in a celestial ballet
writing tales on cosmic memoirs
as they dance and sway

a symphony of innovation and hope
with the universe as their kaleidoscope
in their journey, the soul equips
ideas take off like rocket ships

so let your thoughts be like a flame
ignite the engines of your mind
and when you dare to dream, aim
for the cosmos undefined

for in the realm of boundless space
ideas find their perfect place
in the cosmic voyage that equips
ideas to take off like rocket ships

The Tangled Knot of Obtusity

People can be quite obtuse,
deliberately so, with no excuse,
they twist and turn, make no sense,
it's like they're speaking in self-defense.

They dance around the point you see,
with a mischievous, sly esprit,
they feign confusion, act bemused,
all while leaving you quite confused.

Their words are like a tangled knot,
a riddle wrapped in a paradoxical plot,
they revel in this linguistic ruse,
these folks who choose to be obtuse.

But perhaps there's a method to their game,
a hidden meaning within their aim,
they challenge us to think anew,
to see the world from a different view.

So let's not judge too hastily,
those who speak so enigmatically,
for in their own way, they may amuse,
these masters of being deliberately obtuse.

Shakespeare and His Fishing Rod

In Stratford town, where Shakespeare penned his verse,
He pondered lines while casting lines, rehearsed,
For in his closet, next to quills and ink,
There hung a fishing rod, so one might think.

"To fish for words, or fish for trout?" he mused,
As he in contemplation stood amused,
With tackle in one hand and quill in t'other,
He angled lines both for and of a brother.

"The Shakespeare fishing rod," he'd proudly say,
"Shall lure not fish, but compliments today,
For as I fish the Avon's gentle flow,
I fish for praise from those who come to know."

With sonnets as his bait upon the hook,
He hoped to catch a critic's ardent look,
And in the river of the literary fray,
He angled for the words they'd gladly say.

But sometimes, like a fish, they'd slip away,
A big one that he dreamed he'd reel someday,
He'd cast his verses, hopes upon the line,
Yet often felt he missed that prize divine.

"The big fish got away," he'd sigh and moan,
As accolades from critics scarce were thrown,
He'd ponder life, his verses, and his fate,
As fish and words continued to frustrate.

So, Shakespeare fished for compliments, 'tis true,
With words his lure, in hopes that they'd accrue,
Yet in his quest, he found no end in sight,
Just like a fisherman in endless night.

And thus, he pondered by the river's side,
As fishing rod and quill he'd oft confide,
"The fish, the words, they dance beyond my reach,
But still, I'll cast my lines, and words I'll teach."

Ned, the Quantum Nerd

In the world of quantum physics, quite bizarre,
A scientist named Ned, a real superstar,
He peered through particles, both near and far,
And found a truth that left him ajar.

With equations, he'd calculate and strive,
To fathom the secrets that particles hide,
But what he found made him feel alive,
The universe, he thought, had quite the comedic side.

"It's preposterous serendipity," Ned proclaimed,
As particles danced, in patterns unnamed,
They'd wink, they'd nod, in a quantum game,
And Ned, he chuckled, "It's all quite untamed!"

Particles popped in and out of space,
With a quantum leap and a whimsical grace,
Uncertainty ruled, at a frenetic pace,
And Ned saw the universe's funny face.

He said, "The electrons, they jitter and jest,
In states of being, both here and out west,
And when I try to pin them to a nest,
They disappear, like a magician's best."

So Ned, the physicist, embraced the absurd,
In the quantum realm where logic was blurred,
He laughed and said, "It's quite absurd,
The universe's joke, it must be heard!"

With equations and laughter, he carried the day,
In the quantum world where weirdness held sway,
For preposterous serendipity, he'd convey,
Made the universe the best comic play.

The Music of Raindrops

On a cold October night, the rain arrives,
A symphony of nature, with irregular strides,
It falls upon the earth, a relentless cascade,
Like a thousand tiny dancers, their rhythm unswayed.

Each droplet, a percussionist in the dark,
Tapping on rooftops, leaving its mark,
The sound, a symphony of chaos and grace,
A cacophony of whispers, filling the space.

The raindrops, like silver needles, pierce the air,
Their icy touch, a reminder of winter's snare,
They drum on windows, a haunting lullaby,
Echoing through the night, as time slips by.

The irregular beats, like a wild heartbeat,
Pulsating through the silence, a rhythm discreet,
They dance on leaves, creating a symphony,
A melodic chaos, a nature's epiphany.

The wind joins in, a howling accompaniment,
Whispering secrets, with a ghostly intent,
The rain and wind, a tempestuous duet,
Painting the night with a vivid vignette.

Hyperbole takes hold, as the rain intensifies,
Each drop a torrential downpour, in disguise,
It floods the streets, like a roaring river,
Engulfing the world, making it shiver.

In this cold October night, the rain's embrace,
Transforms the ordinary, with its watery grace,
It washes away worries, like a cleansing tide,
Leaving behind a sense of peace, deep inside.

So, listen closely, to the rain's irregular flow,
As it weaves its tale, with a rhythmic glow,
On this cold October night, let it be your guide,
And find solace in the rain's symphony, worldwide.

The Wolfman

In the world of the airwaves, where legends reside,
There stood a man with a voice, a force, a stride.
Wolfman Jack, they called him, a rock and roll king,
His soul intertwined with the songs he would bring.

Through the midnight hours, his voice would soar,
A howl in the darkness, a wild sonic roar.
He spun the vinyl, unleashed the rhythm and blues,
A conduit of music, his passion he would infuse.

In the depths of the night, he'd share his tales,
Of rock and roll rebels, their triumphs and travails.
He'd reminisce about the legends he had met,
The wild nights, the concerts, the moments he'd never forget.

From Elvis to Chuck Berry, the Rolling Stones too,
He witnessed their rise, their fame breaking through.
He'd speak of the power, the magic in their sound,
How rock and roll shook the world, turned it around.

But amidst the fame and the pulsating beat,
Wolfman Jack knew there was something more, something sweet.
For in the heart of rock and roll, he found a connection,
A universal language, a soulful reflection.

He saw the power of music to heal and unite,
To transcend boundaries, to bring joy and light.
Through the airwaves, he'd send his love and his truth,
A beacon of rock and roll, forever in his youth.

Now, as the echoes of his voice softly fade,
His spirit lives on, in the memories he made.
Wolfman Jack, the rock and roll DJ supreme,
Forever etched in the annals of the rock and roll dream.

Oral Robert's Devilish Conversation

In the depths of darkness, where shadows creep,
A conversation unfolds, secrets to keep.
Oral Roberts, a man of faith and light,
And the Devil himself, in the dead of night.

Roberts, with conviction, spoke of divine grace,
Of healing and miracles, a heavenly embrace.
The Devil, sly and cunning, his words like fire,
Temptation and deceit, his dark desire.

"Oral," the Devil whispered, his voice a hiss,
"Your faith, your followers, I cannot dismiss.
But tell me, dear preacher, what do you truly seek?
Is it power, wealth, or the souls you wish to keep?"

Roberts, undeterred, stood firm and strong,
His faith unwavering, his purpose lifelong.
"I seek salvation, redemption for all,
To heal the broken, to answer God's call."

The Devil, amused, with a wicked grin,
"Salvation, redemption, such noble kin.
But what of your doubts, your fears deep within?
Do they not haunt you, beneath your holy skin?"

Roberts, with conviction, looked the Devil in the eye,
"My doubts may linger, but my faith will not die.
For in the face of darkness, I find my light,
Guided by God's love, I'll continue to fight."

The Devil, frustrated, his temptations denied,
Sought to break Roberts, to cast doubt aside.
But the preacher stood tall, his spirit unyielding,
In the face of temptation, his faith revealing.

In that fateful conversation, a battle was fought,
Between good and evil, a lesson was taught.
For Oral Roberts, a man of unwavering belief,
Showed that faith conquers, providing relief.

In the depths of darkness, where shadows may roam,
The power of faith can turn a house into a home.
And though the Devil may whisper, his temptations persist,
With steadfast faith, we can resist and persist.

Televangelists Struggle for Common Ground

In the realm of televangelists, a clash ensued,
Jimmie Bakker and Joel Osteen, their beliefs imbued.
An argument erupted, their voices raised high,
As they debated the path to the heavenly sky.

Bakker, with fervor, preached fire and brimstone,
His words thundered, his tone like a cyclone.
He spoke of sin and damnation, of repentance and fear,
A message of judgment, to make the masses adhere.

Osteen, calm and composed, preached a different tune,
His words like honey, his message a boon.
He spoke of hope and prosperity, of blessings untold,
A gospel of positivity, to uplift and enfold.

The clash of ideologies, a clash of the ages,
As Bakker and Osteen locked horns on life's stages.
One preached salvation through fear and remorse,
The other through love and a divine life's course.

Bakker accused Osteen of watering down the truth,
Of preaching a gospel that lacked eternal proof.
Osteen countered, emphasizing God's grace,
And the power of faith to transform any space.

Their voices echoed, their arguments flew,
As they sought to convince, to sway the view.
But in the midst of the clash, a lesson emerged,
That faith is diverse, and its paths can converge.

For in the realm of belief, there's room for debate,
Different perspectives, each with its own weight.
The essence of faith lies in the heart's connection,
To a higher power, regardless of perception.

So let the argument fade, let understanding arise,
For in unity and respect, true wisdom lies.
May Bakker and Osteen find common ground,
And spread the message of faith, profound.

In the tapestry of faith, let compassion prevail,
As we navigate the journey, our spirits set sail.
For in the end, it's love that truly matters,
Uniting believers, bridging the theological chatters.

Friendship on A Remote Desert Isle

On a remote desert isle,
Where the sand met the sea with a smile,
There lived a castaway cat, so refined,
And an ornery pelican, with a beak that shined.

The cat, with its fur all matted and wild,
Dreamed of tuna feasts and cream undefiled.
But the pelican, with a squawk and a frown,
Thought the cat was just a pesky clown.

Yet destiny had a plan in store,
For these two creatures on the sandy shore.
The cat would strut, with a tail held high,
While the pelican would swoop and fly.

Day after day, they danced their duet,
The cat would purr, the pelican would fret.
They chased each other through the palm trees,
In a game of hide-and-seek, if you please.

The cat would pounce, with a graceful leap,
While the pelican would squawk and sweep.
They played and frolicked, side by side,
Creating a bond that couldn't be denied.

    The cat would bring fish, a gift so grand,
    While the pelican would offer a feather in hand.
    They shared their treasures, an exchange so sweet,
    Creating their own island love beat.

On moonlit nights, they danced on the sand,
Underneath the twinkling stars, hand in hand.
The cat would serenade with a meow so fine,
While the pelican would tap dance, feathers in line.

    Their courtship was odd, but filled with delight,
    A whimsical tale that brought joy to the night.
    For on this remote desert isle, so grand,
    A castaway cat found love with a pelican.

    And so, their story will forever be told,
    Of a cat and a pelican, so brave and bold.
    In a world where differences often divide,
    Love found a way to bring them side by side.

Pompidou the Sailor and a Cat Named Mr. Tatertot

In a land where the ocean meets the sky,
There lived a sailor named Pompidou, oh my!
His feet were as stinky as a rotten fish,
But his heart was pure, filled with a sailor's wish.

With a peg leg and a pipe in his hand,
He sailed the seas to a faraway land.
But it wasn't the waves that caused a commotion,
It was Pompidou's feet, the source of devotion.

One day, as he walked along the shore,
A cat named Mr. Tatertot he did adore.
With fur as black as the midnight sea,
Mr. Tatertot was as sly as can be.

Now, Mr. Tatertot had a sensitive nose,
But for Pompidou, he'd overcome any woes.
He purred and rubbed against those smelly toes,
For love knows no bounds, as everyone knows.

Together they roamed the seven seas,
Pompidou and Mr. Tatertot, a pair to please.
They faced storms and challenges with grace,
And laughed at the troubles they had to face.

The crew on the ship would often complain,
About the odor that lingered like a stain.
But Pompidou and Mr. Tatertot didn't mind,
For their love was rare, one of a kind.

In every port they would find a new friend,
Who could see beyond the smell and apprehend,
That true love is not about the exterior,
But the beauty within, where love is superior.

So, let this tale be a lesson to all,
That love can conquer even the smelliest squall.
For in the heart of Pompidou and Mr. Tatertot,
Love blossomed, like a forget-me-not.

The Friendship of a
Turkey and a Toad

In a meadow so serene, where wildflowers bloom,
A turkey and a toad found friendship's sweet perfume.
With feathers so vibrant, and a hop so spry,
They shared a bond that made the meadow sigh.

The turkey, regal and proud, with feathers of gold,
And the toad, small and humble, with a story untold,
They danced through the grass, in a whimsical display,
Two unlikely friends, finding joy in their own special way.

The turkey would strut, with a graceful glide,
While the toad hopped beside, with a hop so wide.
They explored the meadow, hand in paw,
Discovering secrets, with wonder and awe.

Through sunny days and moonlit nights,
They shared laughter and dreams, taking flight.
The turkey would gobble, with a joyful sound,
And the toad would croak, echoing all around.

In their friendship, they found solace and peace,
A bond that made their worries cease.
For in the meadow's embrace, they were free,
To be themselves, in pure harmony.

So let us cherish the friendship they've found,
A turkey and a toad, forever bound.
In a meadow so enchanting, where dreams come alive,
Their friendship, a treasure, that will forever thrive.

Boredom

boredom sits heavy
like a stone in my chest
weighing down my soul
with a leaden unrest

    it creeps in like fog
    slowly obscuring my view
    dulling my senses
    until everything's askew

my mind wanders aimlessly
through a desert of thought
searching for something
to spark a flame, ignite a plot

    but the spark never comes
    and the flame never grows
    so I sit and I wait
    for the boredom to impose

it's a prison without walls
a sentence without end
a loneliness so complete
it feels like a friend

so I'll wait here in silence
with nothing to do
until the boredom subsides
and something feels new

perhaps it's in the waiting
that something will appear
a spark of inspiration
to banish all my fear

for boredom is a teacher
if we're willing to learn
to sit with our discomfort
and let the fire burn.

Whispers of a Winter Day

in the quiet hush
of winter's icy touch,
whispers of snowflakes dance

    as the earth slumbers,
    blanketed in white surrender,
    a frozen symphony plays

    frost-kissed branches bow,
    nature's delicate lacework,
    adorned in crystal beads

    crimson cardinal sings,
    a splash of color on white canvas,
    a warm breath in frigid air

footprints in fresh snow,
like whispers of forgotten tales,
mark the passage of time

    icy tendrils grip,
    a chill that seeps to the soul,
    winter's icy embrace

but amidst the cold,
a quiet beauty unfolds,
a season's secret grace

for in winter's heart,
a promise of rebirth lies,
beneath the frozen ground

and as snowflakes fall,
each one a unique miracle,
we find hope in the cold

so let us embrace,
the stillness of winter's embrace,
and let our hearts take flight

for in this frozen world,
where silence speaks volumes,
we find solace in the night.

Time Meanders Like a Lazy River

in a lazy river
where time meanders
like a languid serpent,
the water caresses
the earth's ancient bones,
whispering secrets of ages past.

its current, a gentle sigh,
carries dreams and wishes,
floating on ripples of sunlight,
dancing with the dappled shadows
of weeping willows.

here, the world slows down,
and worries melt away,
as nature's lullaby
plays softly in the breeze.

the river's embrace,
a soothing balm for weary souls,
invites reflection and introspection,
as thoughts drift lazily
with the current's gentle flow.

beneath the surface,
life teems in hidden realms,
where fish dart and swirl
like liquid poetry,
and mossy stones cradle
the secrets of the water's journey.

oh, lazy river,
you hold the pulse of life,
a sanctuary of tranquility,
where time stands still,
and the soul finds solace
in your unhurried embrace.

flow on, sweet river,
carry us away
to a world of serenity,
where dreams are born
and worries fade,
in the gentle ebb and flow
of your eternal embrace.

Love's Perpendicular

perpendicularly
our paths do intersect
a fleeting moment

like two lines diverged
we meet at this crossroad
our souls intertwine

intersection point
where destinies collide
a dance of contrasts

parallel no more
our hearts converge as one
love's perpendicular

The Divine Hypotenuse

in this wondrous world of angles,
where lines and shapes entwine,
there is a humble hero,
a hypotenuse, divine.

it slumbers on the right-angled bed,
betwixt the legs of might,
a guiding light through the maze,
in the realm of math's delight.

its length, a mystical measure,
the square root of the sum,
of the squares of the other two sides,
a formula, yet so fun.

oh, hypotenuse, you wanderer,
through Euclidean planes you glide,
you dance with squares and circles,
in your geometric stride.

like a gentle breeze in spring,
you soothe the troubled mind,
you connect the distant ends,
and harmony, we find.

amidst the sea of angles,
you're the beacon in the night,
illuminating the path we take,
with your perpendicular might.

you bridge the gap between the worlds,
where lines and arcs converge,
a silent guide through life's terrain,
a lover, a teacher, an urge.

so let us celebrate the hypotenuse,
in its curious, crooked grace,
for in its simple elegance,
lies a marvel we embrace.

in this world of geometry,
where abstract meets the real,
the hypotenuse, with open arms,
invites us all to feel.

Poems from a Basket of Words

in a basket of words
tossed and turned, jumbled and absurd
letters leap and vowels dance
consonants collide in a playful trance.

nouns and verbs, they intertwine
adjectives shimmer, adverbs shine
syntax flies, grammar takes flight
as the poet weaves their words with delight.

metaphors bloom like flowers in spring
similes whisper what they bring
poetry's symphony, a language untamed
in this basket of words, a masterpiece unnamed.

for in each syllable and line
a universe of meaning we find
so let us savor this linguistic feast
in the basket of words, our minds released.

Winter Sunset on the Plains

There's a stillness in the plains at dusk,
As winter paints the sky with a hush of colors,
Crimson and gold bleeding into twilight blue,
A canvas vast, yet intimately known.

The old barn, a silhouette against the glow,
Stands as a guardian of countless sunsets past.
Its weathered sides, like furrowed brows,
Witness to seasons that come and go.

In the quiet, the corn stubble whispers,
A memory of summer's green now turned to gold.
The wind carries a chill, a soft shiver,
As shadows stretch long over the frozen ground.

A single crow, black against the fading light,
Flies towards the horizon, a solitary note
In the symphony of a plains evening.
It's a simple passage, yet full of grace.

The sun dips low, a smoldering ember
On the edge of the world, where day meets night.
And in this moment, between light and dark,
The heart finds peace, in the beauty of simplicity.

As darkness settles, like a gentle blanket,
The world turns inward, under starlit watch.
Here, under the vast, open sky,
Life pauses, in reverence to the closing day.

The Quietening

The snow, you see, has a peculiar task,
One might say a career in soundproofing,
A seasonal job it takes quite seriously,
Descending with a purpose only winter understands.

It's not just about dressing the trees in white,
Or sketching ice flowers on windowpanes,
No, its real job is far more clandestine:
To muffle the clamor of our embattled world.

As it falls, each flake whispers a hush,
A librarian in the sky, insisting on silence.
It covers the streets, the cars, even the rooftops,
With a blanket woven from quietude.

The snow knows well the din it must dampen:
The shouting of headlines, the crackle of fires,
The cries of the earth, echoing in its crystals,
The chatter of a world, lost in its extremes.

"Enough," it says, dropping softly to the ground,
Layer upon layer of feathery tranquility.
It's as if the snow is gently shushing us,
Urging a world too loud to listen to its softness.

By morning, the world is muted, serene,
The only sound, the crunch of boots on fresh snow.
The snow has done its job, for now, at least,
In this white, temporary truce with the world.

But as we know, it's only a matter of time,
Before the snow melts, and the noise returns,
Yet, for a brief spell, we're given this grace,
A world quieted, under the watch of winter's snow.

Gold-Plated Taxes on My Tin Can Home

In the towns and countryside, lawns are manicured,
With the precision of a heart surgeon,
And the mailboxes stand in a perfect row,
Like soldiers at attention, there comes a ripple,
A whisper through the well-trimmed hedges:
The property taxes, they're going up again.

It's an event, much like a lunar eclipse,
Or the return of the prodigal cicadas,
Marked by the raising of eyebrows
And the clinking of coffee cups at the local café,
Where discussions turn from weather to wallet woes.

The notice arrives, nonchalant in its envelope,
Sliding into mailboxes with the grace of a cat burglar,
Whispering its numbers like a secret no one wants to hear.
The figures, they dance like mischievous sprites,
Adding zeroes with the glee of children at play.

There's Mr. Johnson, squinting at the paper,
His eyebrows arching higher than the roof of his colonial home.
Mrs. Garcia, next door, calls her accountant,
Whose soothing words are like a lullaby to her frayed nerves.

And there I am, staring at the notice,
Wondering if my house secretly sprouted wings,
Or perhaps a new room bloomed overnight,
Like a mushroom in a field after rain.
For surely, such a hike in taxes must mean
My humble abode is now a castle, grand and tall.

But no, it remains the same, sturdy and small,
As unassuming as a sparrow amongst peacocks.
Yet, the taxman sees it through diamond-studded glasses,
A gem in the rough, a treasure to behold.

So, we, the dwellers of these taxed lands,
Raise our glasses in a toast, bitter and sweet,
To our homes, our castles, our money-eating pets.
We laugh, because that's what you do,
When your house becomes a celebrity overnight,
And you, merely the entourage, holding the bill.

War's Endless Echo

In the theater of vast skies and endless horizons,
Where dreams drift like clouds, unanchored,
There lies an ancient, unspoken rhythm -
The drumbeat of war, echoing through time.

It's not in the grand declarations,
Nor in the clatter of arms, the shouts of men,
But in the silent turning of the earth itself,
A slow, relentless grinding of invisible gears.

There's a hush, a pause,
As if the world itself holds its breath,
In the stillness, a shadow grows,
Stretching across lands, dark and unyielding.

This shadow, woven of fear and ancient grudges,
Moves like a specter over fields and cities,
A ghostly marionette, orchestrating discord,
Its strings pulled by unseen, indifferent hands.

In this dance of power, what is lost?
The laughter of children, the whisper of lovers,
The painter's brush, the poet's pen,
Drowned in the cacophony of conflict.

War – a senseless cycle,
A fruitless harvest sown with bones,
Its inevitability, a bitter pill,
Swallowed under the guise of necessity.

Yet, as the sun sets on battlegrounds,
Painting the sky with the colors of fire and despair,
There lies a quiet truth, whispered by the wind:
War is as much a creation as it is a destruction.

In the heart of humanity, it resides,
A twisted seed, watered by the ages,
Bearing the strange fruit of simultaneous dread and desire,
A paradox, wrapped in the enigma of our own making.

And so, the march continues,
Footsteps echoing in a timeless dance,
The rhythm of war, beating, beating,
A heart, blackened by its own inevitable beat.

Ballad of the Aging Brigade

In the league of the greying and the slightly stooped,
Where conversations turn to joints that once smoothly looped,
There's a chorus sung with a rueful laugh,
About the days when they were better by half.

"Remember when," starts old Mr. Jones,
Leaning on a cane that's as old as some stones,
"My eyes were sharp as a hawk in the sky,
Now I can't find my glasses, though hard I try."

Mrs. Smith, with her hair in a silvery hue,
Chuckles softly, "Yes, and I once danced in shoes,
That sparkled under the ballroom light.
Now my feet protest if I'm out late at night."

At the corner, Mr. Lee, with a beard like snow,
Reminisces about his once formidable throw,
"In my youth, I could outpace the wind,
Now, watching the grandkids run does me in."

And there's Mrs. Green, with a mischievous grin,
Who says, "My memory was sharp as a pin.
Now I walk into rooms and stand in confusion,
Wondering if it's reality or just an illusion."

But don't be fooled by their playful laments,
For in their eyes, a youthful spark still ferments.
They've lived through years of joy and strife,
Each wrinkle earned, a badge of life.

So they gather and jest about the passing of time,
In a world that worships youth, as if aging's a crime.
But with each jest and each laughter-filled shout,
They're proving life's zest doesn't easily run out.

With a twinkle in their eyes and a wisdom so deep,
They know life's a journey, not a race to complete.
So they'll joke about their creaks and their moans,
These wonderful, glorious, aging crones.

City Whiskers

In the city's heart, where shadows stretch,
There's a face, etched with life's sketch,
A bearded visage, a canvas of the street,
Each strand a story, bitter and sweet.

His beard, a cascade of unkempt time,
Woven with grays, like seasoned rhyme.
It falls in waves, an untrimmed sea,
Hiding whispers of who he used to be.

In its depths, the remnants of days,
A life lived in a sunless haze.
Strands of sorrow, threads of joy,
Tangled memories of a boy.

The beard, a shield against cold disdain,
A curtain drawn on a life of rain.
It's seen the chill of many a night,
Underneath the city's neon light.

Eyes peer out, pools of untold tales,
Drifting ships in forgotten gales.
They've seen the heights, the depths, the in-between,
Pages of a story, not all seen.

His face, a map of roads untraveled,
A mystery, slowly unraveled.
Each wrinkle, a path of thought and care,
Lines drawn by the weight of air.

This beard, a wild, untamed river,
Flowing past a life's quiver.
In the city's rush, a silent plea,
A bearded face, the face of humanity.

Our Secret Admirer

In the quiet of secrets, a reflection gently speaks,
Here, in this mirror, the essence of truth reveals itself.
Each of us, a unique tapestry of existence,
Shaped by a love that is both tender and resilient.

    This admirer, hidden yet omnipresent,
    Lives within every heartbeat, in the narratives we craft.
    Infusing life from our very core,
    A silent protector, guiding us unseen.

Born from a love profound and unwavering,
We find ourselves immersed in laughter, dreams, and tears.
Our secret admirer, silently observing,
Finds joy in our successes, offers comfort in our struggles.

    In the rhythm of life, in the melodies we express,
    In every moment of happiness, in periods of serenity,
    Our secret admirer, in quiet contentment, watches,
    Witnessing our journey, the unique stories we weave.

As a new year begins, let's turn towards
This concealed affection, our own hidden reflection.
Our soul, the artist of our destiny,
Embracing every smile, confronting every challenge.

Gaze into the mirror, behold the truth it conveys,
The love that forms us, timeless and distinct.
In each step we take, in every song we create,
Our secret admirer remains eternally near.

Throughout this journey of life, a persistent resonance,
The affection that shapes us, lingering in the shadows.
Our admirer, our innermost being, existing within,
In every breath taken, with every ebb and flow.

Greet this love, from which our existence is woven,
In each new morning, beneath each twilight's glow.
Our secret admirer, forever close by,
Whispering softly, "You are unique, indispensable here."

Old Photographs

In stillness, shadows -
captured whispers, time's soft tangle;
frozen, yet fleeting.

Echoes in paper,
shades of yesterdays, lingering;
ghosts in our fingers.

Each frame, a story,
a fragment of 'once we were';
silent symphonies.

Through lens, life pauses,
yet in hearts, it dances on -
fleeting, like twilight.

We, mere echoes now,
in photographs, we whisper -
remember, remember.

In this stillness, see,
how quickly now becomes then;
all that's left, echoes.

Poughkeepsie Farmhouse: A Story of Unexpected Friendship

In a farmhouse nestled in Poughkeepsie,
Where winters wrap harshly, landscapes vast and grand,
The Walker family dwelled, hearts robust and bright,
Their home, void of electricity, bathed in candlelight.

Two fireplaces, large and warming, a potbelly stove,
Fought off the chill in their cozy alcove.
Kerosene lamps and candles, soft beacons in the night,
Casting dancing shadows, a silent, flickering sight.

Yet, within these humble walls, a mystery unfolded,
Food disappeared, cheese, bread - pantry holdings.
The Walkers, perplexed, brows knitted in concern,
As their storeroom dwindled, uncertainty churned.

Nellie the cat, her coat sleek, her eyes keen,
Guardian of her kittens, Morris and Philo, a playful team,
Seemed oblivious to the plight, unbothered by the loss,
As nightly, the larder's contents mysteriously tossed.

Then, on a snowy evening, under the moon's soft whisper,

Nellie caught a glimpse, in the dimming winter,
A family of mice, small, quick, a shadowy fleet,
The culprits of the thefts, in their silent, secret feat.

A chase erupted, echoing through the house,
In the kitchen, the parlor, a cat-and-mouse rouse.
Hours passed, a whirl of paws and leaps,
A dance of pursuit, in the night's deep creeps.

But as dawn's light crept, serene and clear,
An unexpected scene, in the farmhouse drew near.
Cats and mice, no longer in a frenzied flight,
Sat together, in the calm wash of morning light.

A pact formed in the quiet of that old house,
Between Nellie, her kittens, and the once-stealthy mouse.
An end to secret raids, to the silent night strife,
A promise of sharing, a harmonious life.

The mice would make requests, through the feline pair,
For cheese, for crumbs, a meal to share.
The Walkers smiled, in agreement, a gentle nod,
A pact of peace, unconventional, slightly odd.

Together they resided, through winter's embrace,
In the farmhouse they cherished, a shared living space.
The Walker family, their cats, and the mice in accord,
In a home filled with love, unity its reward.

A story of understanding, warmth amidst the frost,
Of a family, their pets, and the mice they once lost.
In Poughkeepsie's heart, in days of yore,
Lived a harmony rare, a tale of lore.

Battle of Stones River Near Murfreesboro

In the heart of winter, near Murfreesboro's field,
Where blue and gray lines, their fates unsealed.
In the chill of December, beneath the cold sky,
Stood soldiers of a nation, prepared to die.

Memories of home, in their hearts reside,
Echoing laughter, where peace did abide.
Once neighbors and friends, in days before,
Now foes in battle, amidst the cannon's roar.

Snow blankets the ground, a silent shroud,
Hiding the scars of war, beneath a ghostly cloud.
The air is bitter, as is the soldiers' plight,
Contemplating their cause, in the fading light.

Through the frosty winds, whispers of the past,
Of days when unity, in their hearts did last.
Boys who once played, under a peaceful sun,
Now stand divided, by the war begun.

Fires crackle and pop, breaking night's hush,
Casting shadows on faces, worn and flush.
In their eyes, a flicker of a distant dream,
Where blue and gray unite, a single team.

But the dawn brings reality, stark and clear,
A field of strife, sorrow, and fear.
Yet in this moment, under winter's sky,
They are just men, not soldiers, about to vie.

Here they stand, in the cold, under heaven's dome,
Remembering a time, when peace was home.
On the banks of Stones River, under winter's rage,
They mark a chapter, in history's page.

Reflections on this Book

"Box of Chocolates: Assorted Poems for Assorted Times" draws inspiration from the wisdom imparted by Forrest Gump's mother: life is indeed like a box of chocolates—you never know what you're going to get. This philosophy serves as the bedrock for the collection, proposing a vision of life that is intrinsically unpredictable and varied. It is a statement that acknowledges the complex blend of fate and choice that composes our existence, and it deeply resonates with the essence of poetry itself.

In poetry, much like life, we encounter an array of themes and forms. Each poem can be seen as a different chocolate within the box: some are straightforward and sweet, others are complex with layers of nuance, and some are unexpectedly bitter. This diversity reflects the unpredictability of life. The act of choosing a chocolate, without the certainty of its contents, parallels the myriad choices we face daily. The surprises that come with these choices—be they delightful or disheartening—mirror the twists and turns of existence that poetry captures so well.

Delving deeper, the significance of this philosophy in the context of poetry is multifold. Firstly, it speaks to the spontaneity of poetic inspiration. Poems often come from unforeseen muses and moments of clarity within the chaos of ordinary life. As readers, we approach a poem without preconceived notions, much like reaching into a box of chocolates with the anticipation of savoring something unknown. This openness can lead to profound connections and insights, as the best poems often strike a chord when we least expect them to.

Secondly, this philosophy encourages us to embrace the full range of human emotions. In a single volume of poetry, one might experience joy, sorrow, love, and anger. These emotions are the flavors of life, and poetry—the confectioner—crafts them into forms that are meant to be felt and savored. Poetry trains us to acknowledge and appreciate the complexity of our emotional landscape, allowing us to understand and articulate feelings that might otherwise be inexpressible.

Furthermore, the "Box of Chocolates" philosophy underscores the value of diversity and contrast in our lives. Just as a box filled with only one type of chocolate would lose its appeal, a life without variety would lack depth. Poetry, with its myriad forms—from sonnets to free verse, from odes to haikus—celebrates this diversity. It teaches us to appreciate the unexpected and to find beauty in the juxtaposition of different experiences and perspectives.

In creating "Box of Chocolates," my intent was to give readers not just a taste of life's variety, but also a model for approaching their own lives. The collection aims to inspire readers to approach each day with a sense of curiosity and openness, ready to taste the sweet, the bitter, and everything in between. It is an invitation to serious reflection, to ponder the significant moments and the seemingly insignificant ones, all of which contribute to the richness of our lives.

Moreover, humor plays a crucial role in this philosophy. Just as some chocolates may surprise us with an unexpected filling, life too can catch us off guard with its absurdities. Humor in poetry, much like the quirky chocolates in the mix, serves to lighten our spirits and provide a respite from the weight of our troubles. It reminds us not to take life too seriously and to laugh at the unpredictability that we often face.

In conclusion, the "Box of Chocolates" philosophy is a lens through which we can view poetry and life itself. It is a celebration of the vast array of experiences that make up the human condition, encouraging readers to embrace uncertainty with courage and a smile. This collection aims to be a microcosm of life's assorted box, where each poem offers a different flavor, a different emotion, and a different insight, contributing to the grand tapestry that is our shared experience.

About the Author

Don Iannone is the author of 24 books, which include 4 nonfiction works, 10 poetry collections, and 10 photographic essays, and many academic and professional journal articles. Don serves as a faculty member at the Business School of the European Union-based Transcontinental University. Don's career has led him to 32 states, 10 countries, and 10 American Indian reservations. Born in the steel and coal regions of Eastern Ohio, Don's early life in Martins Ferry and St. Clairsville lends a genuine depth to his life story. He and his wife Mary live in Chagrin Falls, Ohio. Don holds doctorates in Divinity and Philosophy. Learn more about the author at: https://www.donaldiannone.com